I0079471

FOUR RAVENS

ALSO BY
GARY LEE ENTSMINGER

Ophelia's Ghost
Remembering the Parables
Making the Most of WriteItNow 4
Fall of '33
Two Miles West

FOUR RAVENS

POEMS

GARY LEE ENTSMINGER

PINYON PUBLISHING

Montrose, Colorado

Copyright © 2019 by Gary Lee Entsminger

All rights reserved. Except as permitted under the U.S. Copyright Act of 1976, no part of this publication may be reproduced, distributed, or transmitted in any form or by any means, or stored in a database or retrieval system, without the prior written permission of the publisher, except for brief quotations in articles, books, and reviews.

Drawings & Design by Susan Entsminger

First Edition: June 2019

Pinyon Publishing
23847 V66 Trail, Montrose, CO 81403
www.pinyon-publishing.com

Library of Congress Control Number: 2019942322
ISBN: 978-1-936671-57-1

FOR SUSAN

& GARCIA

ACROSS THE FIELDS ...

Across the sky, the clouds move,
Across the fields, the wind,
Across the fields the lost child
Of my mother wanders.

Across the street, leaves blow,
Across the trees, birds cry—
Across the mountains, far away,
My home must be.

—Hermann Hesse
Translated from the German by James Wright

tangle 8·2·18
sue

CONTENTS

I. HITCH A RIDE

II. HOLD SPIRITS

III. MORNING DEW

IV. FINDING A RAVEN'S FEATHER

crok
crock
rock
rock
krok

2.15.19

I. Hitch a Ride

FINDING THE WAY

Eva asked her grandfather

—how do bees find honey
—they follow each other
—but how do they know who to follow

part of the mystery had been solved
by Karl von Frisch in Germany
who called it round and waggle dance

Eva read
—honey bees
follow their sisters

into the narrow quarters of the hive
and memorize a dance that encodes flowers
and places into movements

a dance verified by sisters before
who had borne the news of richness
in glides and figure eights

COWGIRL

The wind brought gifts
we had not known
high mountain slopes
where a maiden roams

with walking stick
along a path
in pheasant feathered
felt derby hat

misplaced perhaps
or meant to be
alpine chic
and lengthy curves

she stops and sits
on a lichened rock
to investigate a larkspur
deeply lobed

as jersey cows and calves
come near nudging
her long legs
she wiggles her toes

in this gentle range
no one spends
their lives
on indifferent things

she rises now and sings
as the cows look up
still chewing patiently
ready to follow her

down to the milking
she looks across the meadow
seeing something we don't see
and tips her hat to me

CHRISTMAS EVE 1956

No lights
fields by night
road become an icy
sheet we try
Water Trough Hill again
rear tires spinning
a new Chevy
station wagon sliding
left and right
to stop
a little farther up
each time

Dad steps out
in his black dress shoes
examines the road
determined to get us
to the church
for the play
—we need a faster start
and he shifts to reverse
more nervous than curious
Moms says —let's go home
although wanting to crest
that hill as much as anyone

her sister and childhood friends
await as if it were 1941
and Moms is 10
walking with her mother
along that road
toward the church
almost reaching the door
when a driver out of control
clips them
and Grandmother is spun
into a ditch

snow and ice remembering
stories that determine us
as we struggle to picture
the smoky faces
and seeing them now
as we did not before
Christmas morning
my first bicycle
tree lights sparkling
clearly but not before
we back to the bottom
Dad smiling as we accelerate

FOUR RAVENS

Appeared and stayed
parents and young perched
on power poles
then flew across the meadow

alighted on the high gate
where they croaked and cawed
and pranced a little while men
in the evening sat on the porch

once it was cool enough
and watched the breeze and shade
easing summer heat with conversation
about books they held in their laps

as nighthawks flickered
and swooped in twilight
—nighthawk growl
said one looking past

the meadow to the fence
—close enough to a mountain lion
to fool me once soon after I moved here
the other nodded

he knew the story now
and imagined the lion stealthily
along the fence shielded from them
by sagebrush waiting to growl

WHILE I READ
THE GRASS

Rattlesnake stops
arm's length
tongue tasting

I look up
a kingbird some say
can mesmerize

AFTER EDEN

A man and woman
hurried out of the rain
stood under a narrow awning
with enough protection to imbibe
the sound splashing into puddles

who had noticed each other
before
when she responded to a question
the seminar speaker had asked
about the meaning of life

and without raising her hand
as if without thinking
she said

—the sense of the world must lie
outside the world
—and where might that be
—I don't know

and the speaker had left it at that
concluding his lecture with his erudite
twinkle tapping his pencil on the air
as if it were thunder just before the rain started

and the man and woman found themselves
hurrying along the sidewalk together
when he pointed to a cafe and suggested
they seek refuge there

—have you been here before
—no you
—no

they went inside surprised
to enter a hallway
even narrower than the awning outside

—this way

and she followed him down the hallway
through an opening onto a covered patio
within a courtyard of herbs and flower beds
tall deciduous trees along a fence enclosed
a large area of vibrant color
and warmth where other couples
sat at tables eating drinking and talking
while the rain spelled

later she said long after the waiter
had opened the bottle of red wine
and poured their glasses

—if the writer intends
to express herself in clearly legible
and sometimes beautiful script
without any desire that her expensive
lines be embraced by anyone else
her being the process
then why should we voice opinions
in the late light knowing her intention

must be to suggest not conclude
when she writes

  her tight-fitting skirt
  and high heels accentuate
  long muscular calves

as we see
a woman of above average height
walking away evocatively
while we sip our wine
imagining we're in a small town
of brick and cobblestone streets
in France or Italy

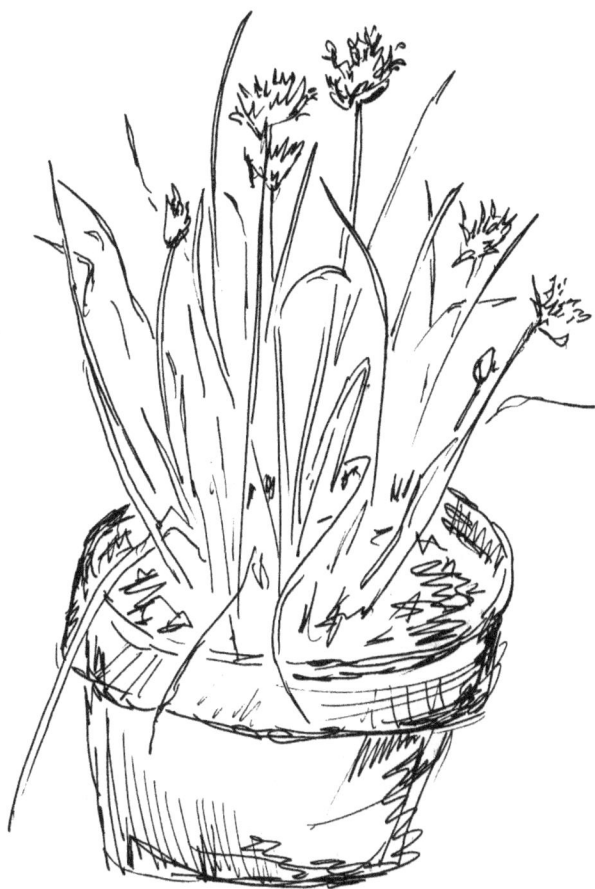

BEFORE CROSSING

In the twilight
waking from a dream
she comes down the stairs
opens and closes the door
and leaves them

looks back and sees
her dog at the door
disbelieving his fate
he has always been
her companion

and wonders now why not
so she unfastens the screen
and he bounds black and golden
like Argos toward the canyon
where everyone before has gone

she multiplies numbers
silently to herself
mathematical singing she calls it
finding roots seeing patterns
smelling pine cones

juniper berries thick
on branches as light trees
she reaches to pick one
turns it with her tongue
until it fractures

she imagines her route along
the steep slope that rises
from Dolores Creek where she stops
to look the way she's come
before crossing

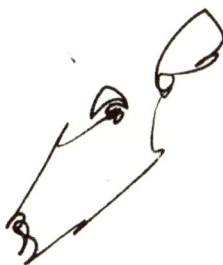

SUNLIGHT

Never draw in anger, McNally
It slows the hand
—Paladin

We were under Sunlight Peak
which springs from Chicago Basin
on the other side

three of us
feeling good about ourselves
when the storm struck

and we rushed down
through wet alpine grass
ducking under a stone overhang

someone suggested cards
to dispel the thunder
echoing like an unhappy muse

around the ridges
but no one had a deck
—we can play without one

someone said
create hands
keep them to ourselves

remember your cards
and try not to dwell
on the lightning

THE BIG IDEA

Was taking the girl farther
than she wanted to go
in a '49 Chevy

like James Dean
wanting to believe
in a miracle

opening the gate
quietly in darkness
easing up

through alfalfa
avoiding tractor ruts
mostly by luck

to the crest of Blueberry
the small town
tucked below

steepled and shimmering
with all you didn't know
in the distance

TOP TEN 1966

High school physics class we sat at double desks
becoming partners in experimental crime
our hands concealed as Chip the basketball star
and I made our top ten lists every afternoon
while Mr. Lindsay explained motion and attraction

of everything to Earth as we experience it each day
orbiting the sun the moon orbiting us and us them
everything moving depending on perspective
everyday new tunes we'd heard the night before
on late night radio

we were too young to drive but loved rock and roll

Cousin Brucie on AM 770 WABC New York City
Dick Biondi WLS 890 Chicago were our heroes
enlightening us with electrifying rambling
Please Please Me and the British Invasion of 1963
Chip slid me his choices I slid mine and we tallied

10 for first 9 for second and on down the line
while Mr. Lindsay dreamed of home
a 19th century house above the rugged cliffs
where the Maury River meandered toward town
the composite of our choices the top ten of the day

a group of kids waited for us outside

as well as I remember we claimed to be the only ones
that listened each night and composed lists of favorites
physics and nudges we couldn't explain
depended on it while we memorized and sang
each new tune that made the top ten

years later we awaited the moon landing
like everyone else who was willing to stay up
into morning hazy TV reception commonplace
but it brought distant places near
to anyone with an antenna

tuned and turned in the right direction
but we haven't been back to the moon in 45 years
more or less why not
weren't we captivated by the mysterious shapes and shadows
that haunted Neil's famous speech as he touched down

one small step for man one giant step for mankind
which played backward seems to say why
—man will spacewalk no
evidence to insiders that something was amiss
but do we want to know or are we content

SET ME FREE

I hardly hear the curlew cry
Nor the grey rush when wind is high
—W. B. Yeats

We rehearsed in the light
of a silvery moon
jazzy snare soulful tune

electric guitar Wurlitzer piano
chords learned well enough
to help friends dance the night away

sock hops where young girls
swirled and parents graduated
in curiosity

okaying how we felt
as we practiced with the Kinks
late at night in our artful bedrooms

spinning the turntable
repeating the riffs
honing the progressions

Paul's clean solos
matched George Harrison's
note for note

insisting he had to play that way
his mom a school teacher
was happy to grade anyone

but she's gone now
somewhere tapping hands and feet
to her favorite guitar licks

WALL OF SOUND

Summer of '74 he traveled with the band
wore tee shirt and blue jeans like the other guys
climbed scaffold to place speakers in the Wall of Sound
happy for the job yet already beginning to understand
none of this would happen again

up and down stacks twenty cabinets tall five times
the height of the men playing guitars on stage
586 speakers 44 amplifiers someone counted
a wall for each instrument center cluster curving overhead
while women down front danced

dresses gliding braless barefeet
barely touching the floor *Jack*
Straw China Cat Sunflower I Know You Rider
tell the folks back home this is the *Promised Land* callin'
and the poor boy's on the line

his first show went something like that
and he worked until the end of the tour
through the retirement party at Winterland
when the sadness blended with unbearable joy
he wanted to climb forever

because he knew there wasn't anywhere else
to go he remembered all the shows
read *On the Road* while someone
drove through small midway towns
to big show cities

Sal Paradise loved Terry
but not enough to become a Mexican picking grapes
in the San Joaquin he repeated her brother Rickie's
mantra —Dah you go man dah you go today we drink
tomorrow we work & Ponzo said —and make a lot of money

we're all in this together & Sal felt it everywhere
and then the wall came down for the last time
and he was back at the farm living with college friends
who didn't know where they were supposed to go now either
in an old brick farmhouse with fireplace in every room

with no hope of hearing them
but a place to remember those last six months
while the images were still fresh he already knew
that forgetting was memory's most devious trick to fool
so he reworked his drawings of the Wall

the ones he'd started that first week with the band
knowing he would never be there again
he splashed the ink contours
with sumi brushes and primary colors
closed his eyes to see clearly

the wall curving closer and closer
—Dah you go man dah you go he said aloud to himself
today we paint tomorrow we make a lot of money

412 BROADWAY

McNally, I'm slower than you are
but I'm not angry
—Paladin

The Stone 1986
like everywhere else
no longer there

humid night
concrete and pavement
marquee announcing

the Jerry Garcia Band
Jerry's back
from his coma

does it matter
that we remember
we were there

Jerry was laughing
up a storm
we're still dancing

CONNECTING WITH THE SUN

With thread and button
she wove a pendulum
to swing

held the thin thread
with right thumb
and first finger

over her left palm
as if dreaming
ten years ago on a beach

while Moms looked at me
from the surf splashed rocks
the week after she crossed over

when I was born
she was nineteen
and would have thought

the pendulum revealed
another world's energy
flowing around us

as we too swing in harmony
to something out there
within ourselves

back and forth
like a planet
connecting with its sun

TROOPER

His cabin
niched into the woods
far from the main road

my girl and I
had been hiking
along the Maury River

cold November eve
as the snow squalled
thirty-seven years ago

we decided not to drive
the long and winding road
back to town

went instead to his cabin
to wait out the storm
the key must have been

in a tin near the door
and I must have found it
I know

we didn't break in
to shiver in that cold room
because I couldn't

get the fire started
kindling wet technique weak
somehow we managed to fall asleep

wind and snow enclosing us
until morning
when the trooper

burst into the room
flashing his light
into our confused eyes

our gloom focused
as he yanked the blanket
we'd found in a closet

exposing us
unprofound shivering
in our clothes

—what are you doing here?
—wind snow bad tires
remembered your cabin

and you unlikely
to be using it
so we let ourselves in

—and couldn't even start a fire
and left the stove door ajar
you could have burned the place down

he said with mock disgust
transitioning to undisguised humor
—not likely I wanted to say

but held my tongue
for a change
fearing arrest

—get up
your parents are wondering
where you are

II. HOLD SPIRITS

GUIDE

Bare shouldered
mountain maiden
plucks melodious
strings of sunshine

drawing the youth
who listens
to her paintbrush

glistening
in a meadow
he has climbed to
dawn after dawn

knowing he's there
she stops playing
sets aside her psaltery

MEXICO CITY BLUES

—For AKB

You start the long drive
through deciduous forests
of magical creatures in bloom
streams cascading with snowmelt
pleasant two lane roads
before you turn into the mainstream
interstate highways of America

not far from where
Kerouac began his first hitch
standing in the rain
with the growing realization
of no ride
and Denver looking even farther
for him

so when he least expects it
you stop when you see him
in wet shoes wearing his backpack
roll the window down a few inches
ask him where's he going
and when he says
you say put your pack in the back

with Ruby she's friendly
but she doesn't want to get wet
you roll up the window
and he gets into the front seat
nose dripping

grateful when you turn the heater up
—what's in Denver?

—some of the New York gang
I'm a writer and I want to see everything
that's happening now
—in Denver?
—well, that's a start. I had to get out
of New York it stifles the spirit
how's about you?

—I have a cabin in the mountains
in Colorado west of Denver
near an old mining town
I go there every summer
I want to know how plants
and animals mostly insects
change from year to year

evolution and all that jazz
—do you listen to jazz?
—sometimes but that's not
what I meant it's just an expression
—hey that reminds me of a poem

By the light
        Of the silvery moon
        I like to spoon
        To my honey
        I'll
        Croon

Love's Dream
By the light
        Of the silvery moon
        We'll ☾ that's the
        part I don't remember
        ho hey moon—

—did you make that up?
—as surely as we're sitting here
it's one of my choruses
to be sung or chanted while
a cool jazzy horn plays

rain falls harder

—I'm sure glad you picked me up
I was about to switch sides of the road
and hitch back into New York
catch a bus
—a bus would be dry
—yes I suppose but it lacks the spirit
of being on an uncertain adventure

—you want uncertain adventures?
—that's what makes life interesting
not just wasting the days
in an apartment on 118th street
—is that where you live in New York?
—no that was long ago

with Edie but I met Allen and Bill there
and there was David's murder
but I had no part of that

as the rain falls and New England encloses
what's behind you in misty glow
you seem OK riding beside this wild
young man who seems to know
where he's going yet not know
inspiring Dylan and Ginsberg
and perhaps one day

you'll name a black lab Kerouac
and watch him swim
in a high alpine lake
thin pure air enticing
—do you have any more poems?
—lots of them
here's one for you about right now

Everything's alright form is emptiness
and emptiness is form and we're here
forever in one form or another which is empty
Everything's alright we're not here there or
anywhere Everything's alright cat's sleep

HALF SECOND DELAY

To measure the voltage or activity in nerve cells
the 64,000 dollar question
—what does it mean to be conscious

in the 1960s neurophysiologists
Kronhuber, Deecke, and Libet
used electroencephalography or EEG

results showing that even the simplest action
such as wiggling a finger or winking an eye
is preceded by electrical pulses inside the brain

that we are unaware of for at least a half second
and thus if our brains act before we know it
who are we

THIS HIGH PLACE

Here
        nothing is diminished
winds howl through the snow
        necessarily

could we have spring
        without winter
would you know who you are
        without memory

the remarkable ones who come
        to this high place practice
an art of remembering to waken
        from the waking sleep

MISSING

Crusted snow shadows coyote pack
howling a dog lost in moonlight
two fawns in scrappy winter coats

appeared beneath the bird feeders
we had been ill at ease
wondering what was missing

26

Rings a bell
when I met you
wildflowers blooming

star-struck mountainsides
jagging from nowhere
rocks and slides

we stopped on the first
ledge beneath the pyramids
which you collected

years later behind our cabin
on the canyon slope
while I wrote this

SPINNING

Earth and moon flew
through the constellation
enticing each other
with high and low tides
drawing us with their moods
and relations creating oceans
everyone spinning
in or out of control

as you point
far out dolphins
leap and dive
we watch from steep
sandy grass above surf breaking
waves and cliffs glistening
in that mist
know we won't be happier

IMPRESSIONISTS

Stroll through a garden
the first one that comes to mind
Van Gogh's sunflowers
or Manet's wooded park
a breeze comes across
the Seine this time of year

honeybees flickering
waves of blue jasmine
people sitting on the grass
you say
—I'm thinking of a color
—red

but how did I know
that color came from nowhere
or somewhere
the color wasn't there
—in the painting you say
in the beginning

IN MURDOCH'S RANCH
AND HOME SUPPLY

Checking out
a heavy-set man
ready to spray Roundup
buckets and thickets
poisoning everyone
around him

he travels up and down the rows
easy to anger wants to kill
but doesn't talk that way yet
something has confused him
he eyes as he plants
poisons for children

long ago people here
knew to grow
sun-loving crops
in a leafy moon
roots herbs berries
learning how to eat

YEW

No one knew
how the yew
survived so long

generating roots
branches strong
some said —mystical

from those places
where poets rhymed
with old magicians

where birds entwine
in branches
singing of immortality

POINTING

If I point
to something
how do you know

what I mean
by pointing
have we previously agreed

that when one points
the other is meant
to follow the direction

of finger along an invisible ray
and isn't speech similar
when we point with words

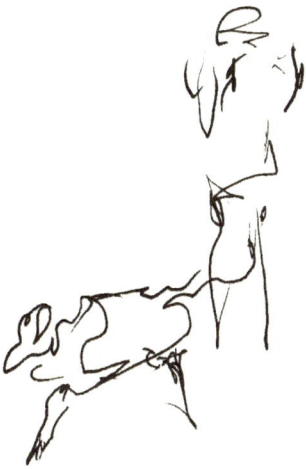

WOOD SMOKE

She heard him downstairs
a gift of her imagination
while she hummed
Bartok's Melodies For Children

the stream by the house
fell into fallen leaves
when she thought
she was someone else

searching her memory for clues
for something that might explain
the sudden wind on her face
as if someone had turned toward her

brushing her cheek
like a Dutch master in old Amsterdam
but she'd never been there
or anywhere remotely European

raised in this life
in the Blue Ridge Mountains
where a number of hollers
met Irish Creek

she'd seen the fallen cabins
knew how they lived before
the water cress flourishing
near the spring

that flowed into a wooden box
a metal bucket and a ladle
which they all shared
idle in a dark corner

she remembered
but had she lived there
or was that someone else's telling
how was she to know

the difference
the wood smoke filling
her mouth and nose
with air no longer breathed

REMOTE VIEWING

The mood reached him
when he read
into a book

a word captured what happened
beneath a moon rising
and his drawings

sketched vaguely
what he glimpsed
as he lay comfortably

letting his imagination drift
while she listened and he talked
on and on evoking bits

of factual spooks
and speculation
a UFO a disappointed housewife

a mockingbird singing
as if the world depended
on song atop a weather vane

they could all captivate him
was that his weakness
or was it something else

rumble of clouds in distance
safe enough away
although spirits are restless today

as the woman he watched
stretched on the floor
leg extended to the sky

hold spirits rest now

III. Morning Dew

PIED PIPER

The eternal sound
draws us near
a land of desires

that we imagine
at least that's how we speak
if someone inquires

for him a place
where mince pie grows
in spiraling gardens

for her a light
that streams from misty groves
of giant redwoods

do you remember
when the piper lured us
with his magical flute

into our dreams
which we thought unique
but that's only how we speak

when unclear about what we don't know
the rats before us gone happily
to rat land homes

ON SIR WILL'S BIRTHDAY

You were throwing sticks
into half-surf
as the clouds rose

those black Labradors
swimming away from you
as you leaned into your white hat

who's to say
where the swimmers go
when the lake freezes over

RAY

Looks older and slower this year
climbing down from his truck
into high Doug Fir

that claims his attention
as he cuts up slope
in rain on Labor Day

the German Shepherd
lying alert and dry
watching him

THE SECOND REALITY

Her braids splay across her sundress
as she sits cross-legged on the wooden deck
drawing lines and curves that become
shapes resembling something

but nothing she can explain
decades later thousands of miles away
eyes closed remembering her crayons
and the colors she preferred before names came

sky reflects through the window
smudges resemble puddles
bright yellow circles simmer
like sunflowers six feet high

as her fingers clutch too forcefully
and the crayon breaks
almost making her cry
her lips purse in silent reply

as she stares at her paper
of many colors flowing
into warm beckoning pools
and she wants to swim

when did she realize her sketches
said something words cannot explain
as objects came together without touching
the way they once reigned

AFTERNOON SOME TIME AGO

Sound of a fan
far from home
twirling

electric blades
that cool her mother's dress
in the muggy Blue Ridge

where people she'd known
want to know
what she'd been up to

the cabin leaving
childhood inside her
as regret hardened

BEETHOVEN'S PASTORAL

Paper browns in an old book
about someone who once took
dreams the way we do

1808 Louie Van
strolls the Rhine
as notes dance

behind his eyelids
coalesce into piccolos
flutes and oboes

pivoting paths of maples oaks
F major B flat Die Lorelei
who tricked seamen into longing

for where the future lies
the way we all do
and must sympathize

birds and rainfelt leaves
ignite his pace
as another idea comes

for a tympani
and a woman who stretches
skin over a bowl

raises her arms to roll the sweet spot
evoking the misty canopy
in an earthworm's eye

GOIN' TO RICHMOND

We crammed into Uncle Raymond's Woody
side walls crowded by dark limbed pines
once Cherokee country

he and his family cut and hauled them
to the paper mill edge of the James River
in Big Island smell it from anywhere

3:00 AM fog rising through gas station lights
1954 or '55 my memory of the year hazy
no one there that morning to ask now to verify

I snuggled into Aunt Katie's lap
Moms much older sister
who couldn't have children

LEAVING TUCSON

Listening to Brahms' Concerto in D
we drive north with sunrise

grooving with gypsies
not knowing what we didn't know

dancing in our memories
when a hawk struck

obscuring the pyramid mountains
as we remembered her

sitting on the piano bench
while her husband played

was she watching now in her darkness
touching the vase of his ashes

OLD FRIENDS

Forget how old we are
the angels look upon us
are we beings

who need them
old friends practicing
intervals and double-stops

octaves of deer meandering
through the meadow
jumping into the garden

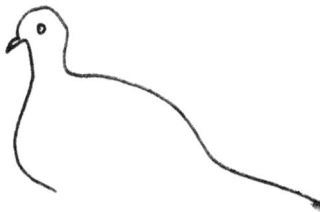

FOURTH WAY

Picking up the old paperback
he remembered when he had read
50 years ago one summer warm
on a third story porch
looking out into majestic oaks
at his friend's house in town
who handed it to him saying
—you must read it

and he started that twilight
mesmerized by a time
when he often spent a night
with one friend or other
talking until next morning
about philosophy music and girls

In Search of the Miraculous
Ouspensky echoed Gurdjieff
designating a method
for understanding who we are
the Fourth Way
as they talked into their nights
in 1916 while watching the barges go by
loaded with wooden crutches

prepared for the maimed young men
who would soon make their exits
from the war that dreadful way
another of the centuries' examples
of man's robotic inclination
and inability to understand himself

a Fourth Way advocates mental
and physical exercises rather than blind
faith or materialistic limitations
to discover our path to immortality
finding the way and not being sold
how to develop a soul
which doesn't come naturally
but requires self-awareness

yet another century later streets
crowd us with machine-like humans
devices and entertainments that demand
we tweet or cheat like everyone else
as the wind blows more wars
and mean spirits lacking compassion
where only those who desire change
find a way out of the madness

VIREO

—For seee

She followed the small bird
as he flitted from tree to tree
between the high branches

always too quick for her
to see clearly
its song unmistakable before

but now less certain
as the air went suspiciously silent
as the weight of the sun

distracted her with shadows
between bright beams
where something seemed

to move larger and quieter
than a bird leaving
mysteries in its wake

which she followed now
as if she were a young girl
going where instinct

commanded her
into another unplanned phase
which always led

to the best sightings
where indistinct edges
dance with light

IV. FINDING A RAVEN'S FEATHER

.

LISTENING TO LISZT
AND CHOPIN

I. Liszt

Who are we
how can we trust each other
with respect not anger or contempt
I close my eyes and do not initiate
any image instead silently watching
what happens next

is consciousness distinct from images
or is it as Aristotle said
consciousness equals them
if I could talk to myself
and deliberately avoid images
would that be consciousness

as I sit as quietly as a rabbit
sensing a bobcat perhaps
without talk or images
who am I then
am I the one who reminds myself
or someone else

II. Chopin

At her dining room table
which is never used for dining
she and her guests always eat
at the kitchen table by the stove

she organizes her book
hand written pages of memories
into a set of letters
to her great granddaughter

the young woman sitting across from her
a poet come down from the mountains
into the desert to type pages
while the old woman reads from her notes

a century almost of memories
and ideas she believes true
and who's to argue
not the young poet

except she does question
an image or the expression of it
from time to time
and the old woman pauses now to think

earlier night after night
before the young woman's arrival
she had sat at a small desk in her bedroom
writing into the early morning

the midnight hour a respite from unwanted noise
a comforting pastoral where dreams awake
as she went into her imagination
seeing how the images wanted

even demanded to get out and onto paper
while there was time
remembering now something
he had said about Yeats

that he was not content until
he at least reached home
in the evening and sat
with his pen and paper by candlelight

her face suddenly full of life
remembering what she had not before
and knew as she heard the thunder
that meant needed rain in the desert

still inside herself with her muse
and wondering who this other one
who was just like her came from
until the young woman gently called her back

and then she said —that's right
it was always the two of us
under the grand piano I was never alone
Mom was always playing

I call to the mysterious one who yet
shall walk the wet sands by the edge of the stream
and looks most like me
(Per Amica Silentia Lunae, Yeats 1917)

IN MEMORIAM: AUNT JEAN

Can we be
like the compassionate ones
Socrates and Jesus come to mind

possibility or mirage
that we can behave better
respecting paths not our own

the woman in the room with me
practices Tai Chi
before a fire in the woodstove

which kept us warm
on the many Sunday afternoons
when our dead friend called

to discuss poetry
and philosophy at 2:00
her appointed hour

but today it's only me
anticipating
what she will say next

SLAVERY

Why don't we examine
our claims to dominance
while the jay calls
from the pinyons near the canyon

as a flicker's sudden
appearance startles us
a mourning dove echoes
far away softly

where no name's song
fulfills the free sky
where we all come together
by and by

OAK

Pâté done he glances out the window
sees the girl still building trail
work not easy but satisfying

attention focusing her energy
as the waning light casts
shadows of unfamiliarity

she picks up her tools
and goes to the woodpile
stacks the oak

looks at him
through the window
already smelling smoke

BLACK HEADED
GROSBEAKS

How long
does a bird
live

we know when
the grosbeaks
arrive each May

they will stay
the summer
above the valley

do they remember us
or recognize
something else

SPRING HOUSE DOOR
LEFT OPEN

Awaits
now what
axes along

debate
well the into
deep go you

crying stop can't
moods these
get you when

bucket love
hole a got you
say you

you say
you got a hole
love bucket

when you get
these moods
can't stop crying

you go deep
into the well
debate

along axes
what now
awaits

JUST WANDERING STILL

Red rocks and fragments of bone
the dog wheel turns

spooning spokes of sand
big stone at the base

flat angled anchor
dog forehead

triangular stone placed
steady gentle eye

white shell barely touching
third eye

invincible as the sand
rearranging herself

MOONLIGHT

Above the plateau
four ravens zigzag
to Venus

WHEN NOVEMBER BENDS GRAVITY

—For JJ & CP

He dreams the Dead drumming up spirits
spinning riffs in a once only show
late fall far from the snow
Tucson November 1969 and he had a ticket

gila woodpecker hammers the saguaro
a beat she learned from Mickey last night
which he picked up in the heat
of feathers in a jungle blur

inside the casita bowls echo
Gaia embedded in clay creaks and groans
dawn silver sliver Moon draws up Jupiter
and Venus then disappears into sunlight

he hears a hot chili pepper harmonica
tearing through velvet mesquite
unleashed bass rhythm of great horned owl
he rolls out of his sack and howls back to coyote

laces his marathon trainers and starts up the trail
a lifetime later pauses at a slow moving stream
wind rushing through pink granite boulders
rippling yellow leaves showering salty skin

pulse of lapping water from the sapphire pool
he sees the border collie eyeing him knowingly
cocks her head leaps through the thicket
dodging cholla leading him on to the next show

SHIMMERING

A chickadee
crashes into our window
lands at my feet
air vibrating
porch board quivering
with delicate weight

momentous moment of reflection
when wildlife can disappear
into our unknowing
where we tell ourselves
that what we've always believed
must be believable

yet the bird breathes a little
I incant softly at first
—remember your good ole days
as you shimmer there
when your friends and you flew
among the sunflowers

KEEPING MY BALANCE
WHILE I WAIT

The photo transports me
to a track near our condo
where I went every three thousand
miles to get the oil changed
in our small car

I walked the rail beside the woods
a housing development between the leaves
beyond the fence always looked abandoned
everyone at jobs school or playing golf
lawns mowed and weeds tended

and farther I see my aunt no longer
90s bent to her garden digging Irish potatoes
near a shed where she kept flower pots
seven winding miles from town
she never learned to drive

SANDALS

She crochets sandals
from thick twine
the snow melting
into the dirt outside
and the sandals
will be ready
when the ground
turns dusty
in spring

waves of energy
rise from the ground
into the soles
of our feet
a friendly charge
from Gaia
but we usually retreat
into hard resistance
shoes that neutralize
the vibrations

Indians knew
to walk in harmony
in moccasins
letting the vibrations
from their feet
alert the snakes
to slither elsewhere
feel the earth
from the soles
into your soul

she pulls to tighten
the stitch
a spool of jute
rolls near her feet
her hands and eyes
engaged
in the love of work
a flute sings
from a distant canyon
echoing her feat

CROSSING

Her notes spiraling
she lifts the pen
and poses the question
to her self's shadowy crossing
—how do I understand
what I've become
when overcome
with reckless news
instead of reckless love

machine-gun headlines
shoot into her headphones
as someone interrogates the sputter
at checkpoints across the globe
every day something new
and action-packed so it gets to
your breast bone
and makes you a little shaky

but she wants to know
how this should affect her
thousands of miles from the latest war
while she shops for groceries
and says to her headphones
—aren't we tired of this yet
does it go on until no crops
are left to torture

outrage fatigue her friends
excuse themselves
and turn their backs on
the daily repetitious information
that will taste like
soggy corn flakes tomorrow

while the raven speaks forgotten lore
finding her memory
—come closer to the farmhouse door
she looks out into a twilight breeze
cool and beckoning
—come closer walk toward
the elderly white oaks
that have anchored the yard
since long before

THE ARTIST'S HAND

Collapses pen flattened
his model not as erotic
as she once was

toes feet ankles
long delaying legs
dance into the shadows

drawing him with her
where it doesn't matter
what he thinks he's used to

her back arches into the sky
crackling for a storm brew
above a grove of aspen

she relaxes her shoulders
he caresses the pen
scratching her lines

SONORAN PASTIME

He's been sitting
since time
pierced his eyes

a plain descending
to the horizon's
rippling waves

he tries
to understand
where the living are

can there be life
without other life
is he alive

the shimmering waves
never rising higher
than his eyes

COUNTER INTUITIVE

My uncle put a gun
on the table
I thought hard about that
as I walked along the Maury River
in morning darkness
with the newspaper bag
slung over my shoulder

people on the other side
of the world are upside down
relative to us
and people on the other side
of the river don't cross over
so Dad said I shouldn't be afraid
of what they're thinking about

my uncle had been drinking whiskey
and the humid air
rising from the moldy swamp
engulfed his breath
excluding the weekend
as Moms packed us up
and Dad hurried us out

the river came from before
and flows into the ocean much later
although it seems connected
and if the world had a beginning
what existed before
the preacher is always telling us
to behave or else

we'll be lost in the hereafter
Dad believes that guns
and whiskey don't mix
I'm not sure what my uncle believes
about immortality
or how suddenly the world
changes with a shot

our brains correct she says
the image inverts and we perceive objects
the way we think they're meant to be
I turn and start back
the darkness lighter looking east
as Dad drives us away
in a station wagon

the gun lies there
right side up
although the image
of objects that our eyes receive
is upside down
as if we're living
on the other side of the world

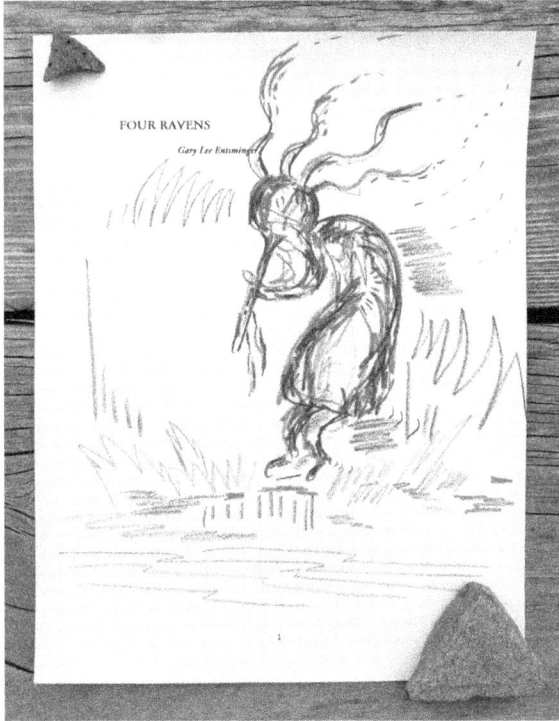

Gary Entsminger is a writer, naturalist, and computer programmer. He has written nine programming books; over 100 scientific and technical articles; and computer software that helps scientists understand patterns of biodiversity and biogeography.

His books written with Susan Elliott Entsminger—*Fall of '33, Ophelia's Ghost,* and *Remembering the Parables*—intertwine fiction, philosophy, history, poetry, and art.

Four Ravens follows his first book of poetry, *Two Miles West.*

www.ingramcontent.com/pod-product-compliance
Lightning Source LLC
Chambersburg PA
CBHW030947090426
42737CB00007B/545